Soul Open

Jeffery Martin

DAXSON
PUBLISHING

Open Soul
© 2025 Jeffery Martin
ISBN: 978-1-966337-02-7
Library of Congress control number: 2025906758

First Edition, 2025

Cover photo: Caleb Keys
Printed in the United States of America

Cover Design by Erica Castro
Layout Design by Erica Castro

DAXSON
PUBLISHING

I dedicate this book to all the people who have struggled with their emotions. Take the time to feel my friends, feel.

Praise for

Jeffery's poetry converses with your soul. Whether sharing his sincere hope for the less fortunate, or condemning the ugly in mankind, his word delivery is as deliberate as it is artistic. His experiences with people, places, and nature are indelibly presented with metaphoric genius. A good writer's message should take the reader through pain, triumph, laughter, empathy, and even time. Jeffery Martin has clearly surpassed this threshold, sometimes sharing his words as subtlety as a butterfly wing beat, and other times like thunder.

Allen Strother author of: Sleeping through the Fire

Soul Open, by Jeffery Martin, is a collection of poetry that will ignite many emotions. Jeffery infuses his life experiences, wisdom and emotion so beautifully in each poem. As I read through each word, I experienced visceral reactions to many of the poems, from chills to tears. This is just the last of profound thoughts and heartfelt expressions from Jeffery Martin.

Carrie Myers author of: Soul Confetti: Celebrating Life's Lessons

Going through *Open Soul* felt like traveling through distant worlds, finding beauty in the mundane as he tells his story with cryptic lyrics to the song that is life. I've witnessed Jeffery's poetic journey before I realized I was a poet myself, watched his growth and witnessed his disillusionment and disappointment as well as his epiphanies and desire to push through. His poetry reminds me of the movie The Sixth Sense where you need to read the poem twice or more times because the ending makes everything else make sense.

subtlety and nuances in every piece, well thought-out reflections that require meditation and few words to convey the message. It's love, it's pain, it's disheartening, it's inspiring, it's soulful, so it fits the book title to a T. Easy to read and understand if you sit still and turn off the noise around. *Soul Open* goes well with coffee or tea. Let it sit and breathe.

Victor Sotomayor
(Theria Entertainment)

Soul Open

Jeffery Martin

Table of Contents

Untitled

Don't lose a poet
the air they breathe
has celestial ties
they speak a truth
that time cannot diminish
using words like love
and hurt, but avoiding on
platitudes which fill space
but are devoid
of substance

Don't lose a poet
for introductions are
rare and fleeting
but tied to the
indomitable spirit
of hope
songs feel different
oceans dance
skies smile
and the heart
improves its vision

No, don't lose a poet
hold tight
for they are like
snowflakes
hard to hold and
almost impossible
to imagine

On This Side

On this side
lies the sun
far removed from loud
voices pretending
there is growth
here in the shadows
yes, the tears accompany
the lessons
but things miraculously
grow

On this side
lies the sun
the road narrow
and thus painful
absorbs nutrients
from the diet of
alone time
flowers are strategically
pushing through hardened
soil
one at a time
but the aftermath
opens soul portals
unimagined

On this side
lies the sun
requesting solo
escapades
where whimpering

floats through dark
skies
and nimbus clouds
pretend to be all
powerful

Absolutely, on this side
lies the sun
where maladies are
quarantined long enough
to show the transformative
powers of wading
through waters warm
and nutrient rich

Where The Monster Resides

It lives comfortably in
the silences
that pretend not to see
feel or hear it
it resides in the burning
calls
that assist in burning
flesh and dreams
it resides in the
unnecessary maze
housed in projects of
grand design
warehousing promise
and potential
in ignorant metaphors
that stand
the test of time
with grand illusions
stating, "This is all it can ever be"
it resides in the neighbor
who crosses the tracks
smiles and laughs often
but never truly believes
he or she is amongst
peers or equals or
humans
the monster looms in
every stereotype
and hypocritical nuance
growing stronger with

every imperial seance
where old habits
never die
but blot out
histories
with one swipe of
its monstrous paw

Eclipsed Sun

Omnium meretricis
and yet I yearned
for the intangible
that poetry
convinced me I could
obtain if love
was strong enough
to disregard
what hid just behind
makeshift curtains
and unhinged doors
and the moans of
ghosts still living
and numerous
most having forgotten
the color of your eyes
or favorite perfume
instead family members
traded intimate stories
about you
in between laughter
and cannabis smoke

Omnium meretricis
and yet I begged
your heart to open
just once to one
who would
never untidy your
presence or reputation
to one who would

remember more than
sweat
late night escapades
when nothing new
lay in the horizon
I felt all the ghosts
competed with them
unknowingly, naively
but I wanted you
and yet it was easier
to leave
because the murky faces
treated you badly
and badly was
your aphrodisiac

(remembering the day that went dark)

*Omnium meretricis, Latin phrase meaning, "belongs
to all"

Quintessential

When the call arises
for the mother of that
true north
without question
your name shall
be mentioned
and held
as example
of what that exemplary
position means

There were no barriers
or harsh storms
embittered enough
to embitter you
your children's place
in the sun
took precedence
over the antagonistic
behavior of poverty
in fact with soft hands
you lured them into
the mindset
that they possessed
riches
enough in fact
to share with peers
who had mothers
but not you

There were misunderstandings
but never misdirection
for you were rooted
in the fertile recipe
of ingredients required
to create
character
resilience
love
faith
honesty
empathy
knowledge
compassion
and the keen eyesight
required to see each
in its highest form

She is the quintessential
embodiment
of torch bearer
and light giver
motherhood finds
its home
in her diligence
and its blessing
in her hello

Nice Guy

The nice guy
is never the first choice
so there is proving
to be done
none of his predecessors
had hoops to get through
or tests to pass
but he is paying for
past transgressions
what was easy
in a past life
has become tedious
time conscious
old, used parts
are given a verbal
overhaul
and he is charged
top dollar (mentally)
for overused
and recycled parts
it is unfair
but he is nice
so it is expected

Admittance

To scream
and no one hear
dealing with the
death sounds alone
reaching for hands absent
the noise is deafening
because it only lives
in your mind
you search answers
to questions everyone
avoids
wondering what brought
you here
to ponder many things
is a distraction
for you know
in your heart
that it is love
and its loss

Unsure

I stand in the abyss
unchosen, yet modified
to teach lessons I'd
rather not gather
I have no voice
in this
and yet mine's is the
only voice heard
cries of, "leave me alone"
ring out though my lips
move not
it is my journey
but at times
fear says
it resembles bondage
but the skies yonder
thunderously applaud it
as a resounding
freedom

A Child's Wish

Time is what
they yearn for
that connection
which cannot be
had by switches
or colorful screens
they don't want
to see the mountain
they want to climb it
with you
yes, time is the
goal
masked in questions
and noise
but they are poor
actors
their motives bear the
fruit of smiles
and restful sleep
at the end of attention

Climate

Cold, dreary
devoid of feeling
frozen hearts dictate
what jackets best fit
from a tiny computer
we gauge the temperature
and smile at the recklessness
of its wind
the mercilessness of its
extremes
reflect on the tsunamis
waiting to pounce on
vulnerable souls
too weak to hold on
to promises
and as scaffolds fly
the under dressed
prepare for impact

The Crazy One

The crazy one
has risen from ashes
inherited from souls
too minute to define
or subjugate
a nocturnal butterfly
his best thinking
came when the moon
blinked
and the sun rested
labeled early
climbing mountains
became an unwanted
skill
but it cleared vision
and gave footing
that only seeing ahead
could produce

Helicopter

I'd like to helicopter in
unrecognized
and pour magic
over neighborhoods
which have forgotten
the candles burning
within them

Hover just close enough
to plant books
in strategic locations
with just a touch
creating cerebral
fireworks

I'd like to helicopter in
and cast a blanket
over eyes pre-occupied
with skin types
and where people sit
at society's table

I'd fly in real fast
so that recipients
would not realize
that they needed reminders
about a love
that should have been
natural

Under the veil of darkness
I'd sprinkle hope
around every window
and television would lose
its grip
for hours at a time

As caricatures would
find real jobs
as real people
and stars would hold
their place proudly
because everyone
would look up

Mr. Chomsky

I settle down
into your words
for they guarantee
that I shall never
'settle down' in the face
of homemade hypocrisies
something in your voice
gave rise to mine
unknowingly you are
that poet
well versed, humble
while roaring like waves
in your attempt
to keep humanity
humane

That Dark Place

That dark place
disconnects your breathing
interrupts your sleep
you walk without direction
and awake from dreams
with tears in your eyes
it is impossible to stay
there for very long
you snap out of it
or you die

Light

There is something
special
about light
that does not
falter in the storm
a resilience
otherworldly
something abstract
about the walk
that light takes
It's not overbearing
but constant
like breath or fall colors
never trying to over reach
it points out stars
seldom seen
one by one

Hopes

I apologize
for dreaming too big
and forgetting that
the little things
were essential
sorry that my foresight
was limited
and the whole picture
took a while
to come into focus
I wanted to find
your golden slippers
but could only supply
socks
your size but
uncomfortable
frustration set in
and I blamed life
you understood
and continued to
believe
that I would find
your golden slippers
too in love
to admit
that the socks
had conveniently
conformed to your feet
you allowed me to
run towards dreams

to be
and you smiled
through the tears
because you somehow
knew those golden
slippers
were a disjointed
part
of what I believed
was manhood
life took us
to different
intersections
but dye had been
caste
I would never
hand you those
golden slippers
but you would give
me golden memories

Not The Same

From humble beginnings
myself
for some time
didn't see my wealth
hated the reflection
staring back at me
questioned my existence
and the mystery
man I looked to
said I wouldn't
amount to much
grew accustomed to put downs
and the violent touch
ran away from the demons
but not through alcohol
or getaway drugs
found a corner
in the library
and grew real snug
expanded my world
and the worldview
learned I ain't what
I come from
but instead what I do
took it deeper
than skin color
more profound
than a name
some of us

built different
we are not
all the same

Connection

True connection
is on a soul
level
it doesn't concern
itself with looks
or race
or social status
there is no time
for such trivialities
because kindred spirits
meet on a different
frequency
there is no competition
or petty jealousies
for they are too busy
demonstrating to the world
where relationships can go
once hearts begin to
communicate

Just Outside

The menagerie
has no lure
thinking kept in captivity
initiates flight
singing out of tune
for appearance sake
has a metallic after-taste
so there is distance
in the distance
metaphors can't explain it
so stepping over
puddles
incites poetry
but by at least
an arm's length
away

Raven

This dog
this little black dog
with a limp
follows me everywhere
like there is sunshine
in my back pocket
I helped her once
and she never tires
of reminding me
that she remembers
but I don't like
small dogs
yet I love her
this dog
this little black dog
with a limp
who follows me
everywhere

Cold Hands

Phone call
from newfound family
was monotone
almost emotionless
while I, barely knowing
you
felt my heart sink
and tears gather
just behind my eyes
they would not fall
but they were there
pushing
the distance between
California and New York
had been the barrier
this time
prior to that
it was ignorance
and lies
you were my father's
brother
My uncle
as happy to greet me
at twenty-four
as most would be
holding a newborn
your hug was long
and not pre-planned
I expected rejection
you didn't know
the meaning of

the word
where had I been
all this time
you asked
"In the dark"
I answered
the secret
was kept well
now you know
you replied
still holding me
we would make up
for lost time
but the pull of
New York
took me away again
yet, not before talks
and barber shop
visits
you were not my dad
but I wished
you were
you smiled more
and now this
phone call
monotone and
emotionless
informing me that
an overdose
had ended your smile
the click of the phone
represented eternity
and closure
or so I believed

but years later
the universe on its
whimsical bounce
put your child
in my presence
and your story
was given flesh
yes, heroin
played culprit
but you had loosened
its grip
by finding solitude
miles away from friends
with cold hands
365 days
you tore away
the old scars
your smile was back
another birthday
approached
and cold hands
tempted you
one more time
they sang
you dove in
smiling
cold hands applauded
until you seized
then cold hands
became calloused
hands
dropping you in
a Long Beach
emergency room

saying nothing
about your shallow
breath
sitting you in an
uncomfortable chair
where you died
because only the
cold hands knew
you weren't breathing

Praise

I adore beauty
in all of its facets
as it rustles
through leaves
mixes with rain
gives substance to poetry
adds balance to sunrises
and sunsets simultaneously
and inspires nature's music
yes,
I adore beauty
especially when
it has nothing
to do with
talking mirrors

A Taste

I disappear
the moment
you look at me
with ill-fitting glasses
lenses scratched,
dirty
and a prescription
known to lead
to blindness
it is not
the lack of vision
that troubles me
but rather
the limited vocabulary
brought on by ignoble
life cataracts
used to define
me

Ghosts

They hide
behind their money
hide their money
live free
and fearful
with their money
pretend with their money
lock and store
with their money
die young and miserable
with their money
or live long and lonely
with their money
judge themselves
and you
with their money
create a matrix
with their money
and the ill-advised
stand at the gates
and pay for entry

Whistle A Miracle

I want to whistle
a miracle
create a calming mist
every time hate
gets rambunctious
play a melody
so beautiful
that separating gods
are forgotten
and wars are
put to death
before they can
cause it
I want this
miracle vibrating
so strongly within
the good
that the bad
have no reprieve
or gun powder

One Size Fits All

Criminal aspirations
glean
amongst this breed
one dimensional
classrooms
park for free
on dark corners
across this sovereignty
news accounts are
put on repeat
goals are minimal
and ghetto mommas
introduce the prerequisites
anyone who can speak
wants to rap
and asian owned
weave shops
introduce brown girls
to beauty
what decorates
the neck,
ear
and pinky finger
is more important
than what encapsulates
the mind
dying to survive themes
play through old
cassette tapes
and waiting is the
national pasttime

wanting to explore
beyond a ten mile radius
is frowned upon
books are used
to support
failing mattresses
and television
is the new Jesus
unquestioned and
anointed
with stereotypes
so poignant
that millions of
white people
believe they have
black friends
with inflections
mimeographed
and used to barter
swag
disgusting until corporations
can incorporate it
into white suburbs

One size fits all
despite the indigo
children
sonically parallel
with galaxies
not yet decipherable
the assumption that
burden bearers enjoy
holding old things
tip toe softly

and lucidly
through entitled
orchards
until black fingers
stand behind them
in line holding
an orange

Fake Prophet

The way he looked
in the backseat
first,
at my brother
and sister
then,
at me
"Don't be like him"
he said gesturing
towards me,
"He won't grow up to be shit"
I almost proved him right

Occasion

For the occasion
the words must
paint the page
like stars
tap dancing
on an anticipating sky
jumping from the pen
like hot corn kernels
right before their
transformation into popcorn
be so funky
that James Brown
comes to mind

Yeah, for the occasion
the audience
must marvel at
the theatrics
while being humbled
by the theorems
lining my pockets
with clever catch phrases
creating a universal
"Goddamn"
in a disjointed world
skipping right past
dumb shit
to my shit
which is "the shit"

The occasion calls

for more than
testimonials
which incite anger
but do little in the
way of solutions
it is all for
nestling down with
profound books
jabbing with thinkers
sharpening weapons
with warriors
the moment isn't here
to be captured
it's here to be turned
into rocket fuel
to reach galaxies
unimagined
it doesn't come
and go
it comes and it stays
praying for those
who step out of
the matrix
long enough to
recognize it

This occasion
is no fast food
get it and quit it
buffet of meaningless
banter
it is that holy ghost
feeling
mental tsunamis

crashing against
stubborn fallacies
perched upon small
brains
enveloped by gigantic egos
great things spilling over
into the physical realm
resulting in temperature
change
and molecular structures
suited for to godly
edifices
but floating close enough
to enrich the observant
playing on asphalt
infrequently danced upon
choreographed with third
eye tendencies
wincing in the face
of matrix treadmills
numbers devoid of
substance
casting caricatures
unable to connect dots

This occasion moves
in the direction
of forward thought
synchronized mental
swims
no longer cast asunder
the map painted
on black skies
in anticipatory celebration

shown the way
by stars who knew
the time would come
as good books have
mentioned for eons
the time will come
eyes open or shut
no preparation necessary
karma aligned stars
are word play
for non-believers

On this occasion
the blind will not
receive sight
but the seers
landscape
shall marvel
at itself

Menace

Whose arms
does he run to
when the world
has made clear
it despises
what it won't understand

Where shall his medicine
find him
when poison
dances in the vise grips
that strangle
not only voice
but alternatives

Who shall hear
his cry
when ignoring it
has long been habit
when solitude
of a peaceful nature
requires his presence
who shall remind him
that every bed
is not sandpaper
and every touch
is not thorn

Who will speak on
his value

while ignoring
the weight
he carries
just choosing life
complex is not
of his choosing
but greets him
like a handshake
to a business deal
gone awry
at its inception

What brave soul
shall give him
his flowers
and ignore
the smirk
witnessed to
too many thorns

Name the artist
that shall
paint the ceiling
above him
with hues
which defy
gravity
and transform
space into cathedrals
of significance

Who shall give
him footing
knowing him weary

and uncertain
what kind of
soul
shall turn
this menace
into momentum

The Frost

It lays gently
upon the leaves
brave enough
to prolong their story
as winter does
its signature dance
the hard ground
saves soft spots
for the spring
she knows is coming
the chill plays music
if one listens closely
inviting new beginners
under a white coat
which warms nothing
but sets the stage
for a heartfelt renewal

Shift

Don't come back
for me
I'll have moved
by the time
you've realized
that I don't
happen often
I won't be
hidden in the shadows
or under socially awkward
rocks
the climate will have
shifted drastically
and the seismic movings
beyond the grasp
of your understanding
no,
don't come back
for me
I have seen
prairies
and meadows
and gardens
and heavens
and awakenings
been witness
to forest movement
seen water so clear
that it exposed my
reflection's reflection
let the wind

take my hat
and use it as
a flower bed
please do not insist
on calling
for your voice
has no echo
under the moon's glow
and your language
befuddles me
stand in your longing
as I grow comfortable
being well beyond
your reach

Hole In The Ground

They will stand
there
offering some prayer
speaking of good times
no one recalls
reflecting on special
moments
that observers will not
know they missed
it won't resonate
with them that they
were never family
nor friend
but there they
will be
reminiscing about
times planned
yet un-produced
they will sing the loudest
cry the longest
as they reflect more intensely
no one will know
they are lying
except you
who are now
a hole in the ground

Momma Said

Momma said that
the country
would beckon
re-introduce me
to myself
that part
which could conjure
up things
wrestle with the devil
and win
see unseeable stars
with my naked eye
she said
the city that
I craved
would give stories
but not substance
said I would
look to the farm
the horse
and the cowboy hat
for relatives
long gone
but waiting

The Poison

A series of events
leads me to believe
that they've drank
from the goblet
the fire has left
their eyes
caricatures no longer
offend them
lost without direction
they smile
and thank a
foreign god
battle scars
once so self-determining
now lean them
towards the murky water
where they bathe
and sing hallelujah songs
running fast
thinking slow
displays with shockwave
seismic movement
my god, my god
they've drank from
the goblet
whose fruit
courses through
generational veins
contemporary
and yet
so old

Within

May I write
you a love poem
give tidbits of
the monumental stirrings
you cause
within me
empty every rose
garden
in arm's length
in order to touch
you
may I write
you a love poem
so vast that
whispers deafen
and silence roars

There

How deep goes
the pain
immeasurably so
I cannot reach it
so it festers there
until unbearable
to the point
where I have
no choice but
to replant
myself and grow

Revealing

If I was loved
like I love
oh how the skies
would open up
revealing heavens
song and cheer
if I was loved
the way I love
my love
then you would
still be here

And

I want to write
it all down
give it to the world
stand back
and watch it
take root
as smiles
come from nowhere
but always land
somewhere necessary

Asking

I knew nothing
of pretending demons
hiding behind bright eyes
soft skin and an enamoring
smile
had no idea
that this was cyclical
and stopped at me
happenstance
I did hold
the special place
believed
but was only
a fleeting moment
in the whimsical
mist of falling
in love
without asking
permission
I danced in the rain
not realizing
the mud about
my feet

Bold

We sat at the
precipitous
peaks
dancing fearlessly
amongst tablets
used as scripture
notation by angels
adorned with crowns
eons in the making
we laughed at
their concern
that the fall
was too steep
and perilous
caution accompanied them
nowhere for love
told stories that filled hearts
with haughty promises
and glimpses of
one garden of eden
after another

Surrender

Beloved
I give thee
my heart
followed by the
breath
that fills my lungs
and the essence
which was mine
until you arrived

Memorable

As soon as you
walked into the room
my heart spoke
a language
unfamiliar to me
I began to sing
surprised by the sound
vibrating from within
breathing anew
life was no longer
a falsetto bouncing
off paint-chipped walls
but now a cathedral
enthralled us
and space was given
to this emotion
so foreign
to everydayness

My Angels

My angels
have not had wings
or stepped from pages
of pious sacraments
they have inhabited corners
and homeless shelters
society has spat in
their faces
and excommunicated them
from temples deemed sacred
their clothes tattered
and unreliable
gave them little relief
from harsh winds or people
they have sat at the
lower rung of a ladder
named "upward mobility"
and yet,
everyone of them
has spoken to me
as if my journey
meant something
in regards
to theirs
no,
my angels
have no pearly gate
stories to speak of
but everyone planted
seeds
and pushed me upward

to a place
never imagined
they did not preach
or shout or sing
sometimes they only
Whispered
but oh my
how it seemed
that I was in the
presence of god

Light In The Room

Mysterious how the light
is uncovered, revealed
ignored mostly
it spends most time
quietly in reflection
of some submerged feeling
unknown
"You are the light in the room"
spirit says
but habitual silence
make words unsure,
unresponsive
spirit says again,
"You are the light in the room"
yet the solitude of
anonymous observation
allows no response
and so it sits there
in contemplation
wondering if a calling
has been lost
the obvious recipient
unaware of the magic
held by existence
but no,
spirit has not mistakenly
convened in corners
of unknowns
it has sanctioned
that soul
in this place

within this moment
carrying these burdens
as the light in the room
no broad announcements
no flickering of ideas
the decision made
lifetimes ago
makes no excuses
only gestures naturally
when claiming,
"You are the light in the room"

(Dedicated to Aunt Dot, who was not my aunt, but in
that moment became a treasure in my soul's storage)

Innocence

It smiles in the
morning
plays as if today
held everything
believes guardians
always protect
does not question
promises given
or lies told
it anticipates the best
of all worlds
and the rainbow
inspires shouts of joy
with closed eyes
only chocolate
and puddles
and playgrounds exist
the clouds never
cover the sun
rain is inspiration
and pain temporary
there are no intruders
on dreams
and every question
has an answer
that has an answer
which leads to a smile
innocence isn't barren
or soiled
or mean*spirited
it is heaven*synced

thoughts
designed for this world
but ultimately belonging
to another

Perception

I don't want
a forlorn tomorrow
instead set sight
on crystals in the sky
which send imaginations
into solo flight

I don't want
a forlorn tomorrow
instead epiphanies
arising from every stoop
porch
and malfunctioning elevator

I want tomorrows
filled with promise
and interactions
which are recipes
for genius
with,
every child protected
by the pact
of community
a place where
diamonds never question
their worth

Brains

Old man was crazy
so they say
when he spoke
folks turned away

Don't look at him
they said
don't make eye contact
cuz if he sees you
he wants you to talk back

I did what I was told
until that fateful day
when your mutterings
brought me into the foray
our eyes met and that
was all you needed
the room cleared
with laughs about
words unheeded

"What the fuck you looking at?
Do you think I'm insane?"
"No," I responded, "I think
you got a lot on your brain"

Now you walked over
ready to converse
and I engaged you
which made matters worse

"Why you here" is the
first thing you said,
"With all your belongings
under a nasty bed?"
"I 'been fighting
with the devil"
I say,
"So, I gave him
the finger
and walked away
been walking these
streets cuz I
ain't got no place
to stay
my home is more
than two thousand
miles away"

Old man listened
shaking his head
then he moved mountains
with the things that
he said,
"You too damn smart
to be here first
of all
but, shit, even angels fall
you can't lay around here
all day it's the law
but when I looked at you
here's what I saw
you got promise
some call it potential
but with that, self belief

is essential
it's eighteen degrees
but the library's warm
go there young blood
to battle your storm
then I tell you
what you do
sit *cho* ass down
and read a book
or two
see what folks
did with their lives
and do something
with yours
and I don't want
to see your black
ass come back through
these doors"

Stirrings

I lift my hand
to a mysterious
phenomenon
I bask in the glow
of nature
rinse my feet
in clear waters
and hum gratitude songs
when amongst the trees
I walk by cathedrals
mosques
temples
synagogues
and churches
as I glorify the sacred
that is found
in the breeze
which has carried
prayers for thousands
of years
I am transformed
through observation
my cup runneth over
and yet my learning
adheres to no boundaries
I garner no riches
but diamonds fall
about my feet
confessing no power
I hold the sun
between my fingers

daily
I am the last
of me
and yet others
shall see the face
of god
because of my descriptions

Heartspeak

She touches me
without being
present
speaks my language
without a word
holds my hand
despite distance
I feel her
in my chest
though my heart
be alone
all dreams
end with her face
while defining
my joy

Don't Play With Me

Don't play
with me
I have seen
the meanness
I am capable of
through other people
I have witnessed
the cold stare
of hatred
been in the room
with distortion
and abuse
I've seen good hearts
turned away
and crowds laugh
at the misery
it brought
I have sat beside
broken souls
too in love
with dying
to desire life

Don't play
with me
I've seen tears
in the midst
of dancing
been witness
to the light
of the moon

speak against
suicide
sat in the
classroom of
the anointed
attired in
tattered ribbons
but speaking with
the tone of gods

Don't play
with me
I've been audience
to souls who
stopped being children
after five rotations
around a faraway sun
interrupted instead
of water and laughter
a cover up
for voids too dark
to find a candle

Don't play
with me
because these
are my friends
we met over
garbage and glass
forgetting the smell
and accepting the
jagged edges
but I told them
my pen would

speak and fight
for them
so,
don't play
with me
for I represent
a second coming
of fine tuned muscle
in no mood
for games

Purpose

If my muse
knew her place
beside my pen
imagined her lyrics
within my song
she would smile
and cry simultaneously
smile for the beauty
and cry in the deep
complexity of it all…
this she would find
is a heightened
form of love

Australian Sky

How many eyes
have shared
those diamonds
cast somewhere
between heaven
and galaxy
who has marveled
at god's painted
smile and promise
of more crystal skies
holding dreams
new and timeless
where have prayers
fallen before acceptance
what throne sitsco
smugly behind
this window
of floating ice
unmoved by rays
of solar heat
which poet
moved by its ambiance
was transformed
into a reflector
of light

Australian sky
hold my hand
and feed my
imagination
guide me

from a place
where trees
sing hymnals
and the kangaroo
watches from
the shadows
blanket this island
with jewels
descending from
the mysteries
send music
from those stars
and watch me dance

Jeffery Martin is the author of 13 books and contributor to 7 poetry anthologies. His first book *Weapon of Choice* won best book of poetry in 2008 New Jersey Beach Book Festival. Several of his books have received "honorable mention" in various book contests. Having recently collaborated on a film script, he plans to submit it to various contests. In November 2019, he interviewed professor/activist Noam Chomsky and from that wrote a book of poetry entitled: *Muse Moments: Poetry Inspired by Noam Chomsky*. Mr. Martin also has a podcast called *Write a Way Podcast*, where he and his guests discuss writing, the arts and life experiences. He is currently interviewing poets and graffiti artists in hopes of creating a documentary highlighting the power of art and poetry. He resides in California, but considers himself a citizen of the world.

Publisher's Note

Daxson publishing was created to help marginalized artists publish their work, so the world can hear their voice. The vision for this publishing house is to help people get their work out there, and not have them struggle finding their way through the publishing process. Everyone's voice deserves to be heard, and we are here to help. If you are interested in submitting a manuscript, email daxsonpublishing@gmail.com. Other books sold at daxsonpublishing.com.